Red Herring

Noelle Darilek

Red Herring

Introduction

This book came to me slowly – like waking up after a long night's sleep and trying to recall a dream.

The distant dream is somewhere among your hazy thoughts, but it sometimes takes a flicker of recognition for the story to unfold completely. Sometimes the story is lost forever, a false trail unable to be retraced, and all you're left with is a feeling of something you're almost unable to put into words.

These dreams can become like pieces of our lives we often confuse with reality – some so vivid and clear, it feels as if we lived it firsthand, like a memory we often recall.

On the contrary, some are so foggy we're certain it wasn't us, it wasn't our story – it was simply our subconscious trying to tell us something in a language we can't quite understand yet. Nonetheless, we try to communicate these ideas fully and capture what was said in our sleeping state as best we can.

We compare these moments to our waking lives, we twist their meanings, we hold on to their feelings. And while they are strong, capable, and dreamy, the stories we truly live are the ones we'll remember for a lifetime.

"Turn the page," you said, with one foot in my story and one in your own.
"What you find will surprise you and comfort you all at once."

– two wildflowers blooming in perfect unison

I could walk through our garden forever and
never get pricked by a single rose.
I could graciously breathe in the scent of
each pink blossom and it would never be
enough to fill the space in my lungs.
I could tiptoe towards the horizon and never
make a sound – let the sky and the birds do
the talking.
I could walk through our garden forever and
even that wouldn't be enough to compare;
there's a garden that's bloomed all along,
long ago in my heart.

– the garden

I hope you think of me
in the silence
and in the rain.

I hope I seep
into your veins
and come out
as the sound
of your beating heart.

I hope you think of me
when you can't sleep
and when I'm lying
next to you.

I hope the sun
overtakes your face
as your freckles smile
and the birds sing loud.

I can't help
but carry you with me
through every blooming garden
and every starless night.

– *to carry*

Forget the crooked pillows
and the unmade bed;
they prove that
you were here.

I'll save these
precious memories
swirling softly in
my head.

— *mess*

You took me to the circus,
and we saw the trapeze swing;
the flying was high,
the performance was grand –
you turned a blind eye.

The lions roared loud,
the elephants danced well,
but nothing so magnificent
ever rang a bell.

Jugglers juggled,
others walked on rope,
but all you did
was sit and mope.

When it came to me,
your eyes glittered with desire,
but even I couldn't save you
when it came down to the wire.

– *the big top*

I stole your song
cause you sang the
words wrong;
you never had
the best
intentions, babe.

There's a little bit of magic in the fall air as the Earth leans a little further from the sun; I can't help but smile when I remember our first days:

Walking into the sandwich shop and seeing you behind the counter with my order memorized.

Movies in your messy room — mismatched chairs, portable heaters, and picking out records.

Ducking into the 24/7 diner, hiding from the snow, long talks on the roof, and your warm glow.

Like a whisper that beckons me home, the soft crackle of a rowdy fire, my heart gently calls to yours, from miles away — they beat in rhythm with every sweet sigh.

The rain starts to fall
(to our surprise)
as we waltz into
the secret garden
one afternoon.

The mountain laurels
bloom,
their fragrant scent
lingers
in the dewy air.

You chase me across the
wooden bridge and
take me by the hand.

Raindrops fall
on your buzzcut head
and form droplets on
my summer skin
as time
stands still,
for only a
second.

We run for shelter,
away from the
secret garden,
where miracles happen
every day.

– *petrichor*

Matching birthmarks
on our right arms –
predestined
to intertwine;
I'll love you
for as long
as time allows,
a crosshatch
in the clay.

Kisses like wildflowers
in a garden filled with
buzzing bees;
callow and wide-eyed kids
with scrapes along our knees.

Afternoon delights,
honeycombs,
over-sized shirts, and
a second-story window
filled with light.

One more goodbye
before it all falls down;
crashing dishes, vintage sounds,
the vibrations of our laughter
is all I'll miss
when you're not around.

– the summer house

The snow is nearly up to my knees, but the streets are empty and the glow of the Christmas lights is warm. The snowflakes lie untouched on car hoods, on front steps, on eyelashes, and mittens. I shuffle through the fresh snow, the wind bites my nose, but I stall at a walk-up with a fire escape. Your wreath's up, your light's on, your car parked, your light on. You always told me I could, but I can't give in to the spellbinding glow; something greater lures me home on this winter's night in Lower Manhattan.

Tiptoeing over
teacups
to avoid
broken glass,
knowing fully
well
they're shattering
behind me
as we speak.

Spread as thin
as my paper skin,
you'll never really
let me in –
pressure can't
always
create diamonds.

Driving through
the desolate desert,
the valley of bright lights
and flashing signs,
leaving paradise
to properly greet your vice.

Lay out your cards,
put on your poker face,
burn up the night
with a single ace.

The neon glow,
these sloppy streets,
this debonair air
with its dirty sheets.

Catch your lazy reflection
in the hood of a shiny car —
one more smoke
before we're all seeing stars.

The voices of this street
carry far beyond its walls;
it's a long way to the bottom
if you plan to fall.

— sin city

Those old wayward nights – the word barely rolled off my tongue, you kissed my open mouth shut.

– single

Bridge to nowhere,
your thoughts
gently tethered
to mine –
let them buoy
and rise
like the moon
in the night.

Teeter on the edge
of tomorrow,
Christmas lights
with their halo-like glow –
to look at someone
like they're the rarest thing
you've ever known;

to let the stares
fade to black,
making not a sound;
young love is best
when you savor
its warmth
in a world alone.

Morning rain magic –
we watch the storm roll in
and the mist start to fall
from your front porch.

You sip your coffee
and we share fresh biscuits;
we're just two kids,
but I want this forever.

– *morning rain*

As the sun set
on Center Street,
the birds perched
on the power lines
fly across
the baseball fields
and the steeple of
the church
into the
peach-colored sky –
and in that moment,
I knew we were free.

– *on Center St. at sunset*

We were never quite a story,
just a feeling,
waiting to be forgotten
with time;

an overwhelming,
warm embrace,
a sensation
seeping from
your toes
to your eyelashes
and twinkling
in the blue
of your eyes.

Blank pages,
page after page,
bound and cut
with nothing to show,
but a spinning head of
memories and remnants
of the feeling of your skin.

Our rare blend
of stardust and soul
ensures something
that can never be replicated
or told through the
futility of words alone.

Our depiction of love
fits the shape of our hearts.

Smother the flame,
let out its final breath;
let the smoke drift into my lungs
and find nothing but places
where you used to be
to fill with their air.

My bare feet
on the cold, hard tile,
watching the last of the drifters
leave the dance floors and bars;

Do they know where they're headed?
Do they know where they are?

Their large silhouettes
slink away
in the
midnight glow,
leaving nothing behind,
but one final blow.

– *cigarette*

I stole the scissors, but you cut the final tie;
it's better this way, not knowing where you
lie.

Her golden locks
tumbled down her
porcelain back;
he firmly wrapped
his strong hands
around the curve
of her waist.

Time moved backwards,
and the stars stood still,
holding their breath
and waiting for just
the right moment
to exhale.

Her rosy cheeks flushed,
her eyelashes long;
he kissed her eyelids
and traced the outline
of her lips.

The constellations sighed
as she gently leaned forward
and met his lips
with hers.

Brilliant light
from the moon
soaked
their bodies,
and the Milky Way
poured through

their veins.

– *the kiss*

They say
life imitates art,
but maybe we
were what
inspired the art
all along.

— *museum*

This little love,
this special love,
this simple love,
like the sound of an old guitar.

This effortless masterpiece
can be drawn with our eyes shut tight
with hands as skilled
and worn as ours.

Being next to you
on those long summer nights
was warm and tender,
slivers of light
I'll always remember.

Slip your arm around my shoulder,
let me gently rest my head,
look into my eager eyes
with the whole world in your gaze –

smile so sloppily
and save our kiss for later;
mellow yellow,
you're just the fellow
for me.

No matter how old
and tattered the edges,
our memories will always be
brand new to me.

I miss Seattle.
I miss the color in your hair.
The changing leaves, the lighthouse
was all that I could bear.

Little bookstores, vintage vinyl,
dinner above the fish market;
nothing could ever touch
our ferry rides in darkness.

Perfect diners,
a chill in the air,
our tucked-away house
among the trees of elsewhere.

Does lightning strike twice?
Does it really matter at all?
Admission is devoid
at paradise in fall.

I'm sitting in my usual spot by the window with my worn paperback and a cup of English breakfast, bow in my hair, rouge on my cheeks; I swear I hear your voice through these walls. Peering over my shoulder out the window, I can almost make out your gray coat, your messy hair, sauntering down the cobblestone streets. You disappear in nearly an instant, and just like that – the hot tea swirling steam, the smell of pastries flowing free; if only for a moment, I know you were here, the echo of a distant memory softly ringing in my ear.

– *coffee shop ghosts*

Eyes shut in the sea,
let the waves carry me.
Their turquoise curves
overtake my body, and I
float into the peachy sky.
Hair dripping wet, waves
crashing above my head;
the sky sets with the water
as the tide carries me to land.
Take me where you may –
the ocean of possibilities
and rebirth;
wash away the past,
and take me to a place
I can float forever.

You're an endless summer day,
the grass between my toes,
the sticky sweet of syrup,
the smell of coffee in my nose.

How will our story end?
Will we tie up our loose ends?
Or will they slowly unravel at the seams,
our future simply a silly dream?

What would I do
if I couldn't wake up
next to you,
the rain singing softly
to the morning dew?

Waiting for the storm to pass,
I always knew our love would last;
just me and you
never worried for the past.

– *forever*

The smell of fresh lilac, sunshine shadows, swaying trees.
Sleepy eyes, fresh eggs, two steaming cups, one hungry cat.
Recalling last night's dreams, popping sugar cubes, bursting at the seams.
Living in a daydream, mapping out a day, toast crumbs on our cheeks.
Sweetly sing your love to me; may we bloom as boldly as the apple tree.

– breakfast on the front porch

Baby cut his own hair again –
all by himself;

It was a slow year,
it was one of those years
where the peaches
and the pears
ripen slow.

It was a cherry kisses year,
it was a year spent strolling
through the garden;
it was a whisper in my ear
and a stir in my soul.

It was a cold water,
warm sun year;
it was a deep cut
and a warm glow.

It was a year
filled with
a soft buzz
and raindrop kisses
in my hair.

Some of the most
beautiful moments
are the most
fleeting –
holding tightly
to their hem;

A kiss, a flash
of lightning,
the smell
of sweet pines,
photographs of views
you take
in your mind.

Places you'll never
go back to,
people you'll never
see again –
(at least not
in the same way).

Moments that slip,
feelings that fade –
but memories that
will stay
with you
forever.

I often think of you
and wonder if you think of me.

I think of the ink
of words unspoken,
the rain smearing
and soaking their pages.

A blurry memory –
one you've since forgotten?
Do you still speak them to my ghost?
Or did she leave long ago?

– *smeared ink*

"Catch the last train to Paris," you told me.

But I can't catch the last train, or the first, or the second.
Your words come like an unanswered prayer and a lily begging to greet the sun;
I fight to tightly grasp what's true.

Our train left the station months ago, the tickets all sold out.
I'm left at the platform with my suitcase and duffle; you're sipping coffee at a café or singing by the Seine with someone new.

Our nights of long walks on the cobblestone streets have greeted the harsh reality of day, and the sun shines a little brighter knowing I've begun to learn how to bask in its rays.

– *midnight rider*

Prop open the French windows
to accost an English sky;
pink and coral blushes
as the setting sun winks goodnight.

Leaving behind effulgent splendor,
the church on the hill
catches light on its steeple
as the streets quiet down
and the shops close up.

Summertime sunbeams,
incandescent hearts
beat fervently in time;
love on fire roams the streets
without a care in its mind.

Tuck away these beaming moments,
this lustrous light –
may it carry you through your days
and carry you through your nights.

– English sky

If summer never comes,
if all we have is us,
I think just us
would be enough.

– *lost summer*

These are the salad days,
full of whimsy and candor;
the sunset pulling at the moon,
the 6 AM quiet in our room.
Dancing in a crummy home,
joy rides into town,
the smell of Mary Jane –
memories all too special
to fade. The summer breeze,
broken dreams, scattered pieces,
but us both afloat. Filling time,
junk food and films, storybook love –
the world tugs at our coattails, the
responsibilities try to catch up –
but sweet nights and summer highs
just mean so much.

– *salad days*

Will you stay with me for now? Will you stay
with me forever?
Will you cradle my dreams, and kiss my
flaws, and promise to light up the night?
With your love, with our love, with a love
worth every speck in the sky?
Will you share my burden and wipe away the
tears and the years before us?
Forever could never be long enough for a love
this full of life –
but we'll take the time we can, forever
tugging at our feet.

– *forever ii*

We danced
a cosmic dance,
the language of lovers
slipping through the cracks
begging for another chance.

The shine
in the short time,
cobblestone streets
and candlelit dinners
when you were mine.

Brevity of breath,
our prolonged prologue,
never to see the light,
dying a slow,
but sweet death.

The long train ride home,
never parting
separate ways,
cheap foreign beers
on the roof,
praying our hearts
will never roam.

But letters unanswered,
empty bottles of wine –
the passage of time
reminds me
it once
was kind.

– Indian summer

Dusk

I sat there
with you
like you were
a child

and waited
for you
to go
to sleep.

The light
sank
over the
horizon,

slow-
ly,
but
quick.

The hills
and lake
swallowed
you up

and savored
you,
just for
tonight.

Specks of light
glistened
and glittered
beneath.

I whisper your name in the night all the
time.
I reach for your hand and your heart.

I long for your morning face,
your sleepy eyes, your messy hair.
I long for the promise of rain
and the violent lightning cracks.

When your soul sleeps next to mine,
it's like they've just returned from a long
journey home,
like they've searched through time to find
the other
and settle in this saccharine season.

I whisper your name in the night all the
time.
I reach for your warm lips, your warm limbs
and take my time coming home.

To be young and impressionable
and full of fervor –
your whole life ahead of you
and your whole past behind you.

To hold love
to the highest standards
and live with starry,
hopeful eyes.

Know true love
won't look quite
like the movies,
know there will be
quite a few storms.

Know love may
feel different
than you dared to dream,
and time may hit you sideways
like the strong northern wind.

Know you'll find your
perfect peace
and move in to a home
full of a tenderness and warmth
better than you've known.

– *to my younger self*

Like flowers yielding to spring –
knowing every word
coming through your speakers
is for me.

Every summer
will be ours to fill
with lazy days
and pink lemonade.

Someday in fall,
we'll open our window
to greet the chilly air
and feel the warm leaves
wrap their arms around us.

Winters will be cold and bitter
(just the way we like them)
and teach us how to embrace
the heat of the fire
and the promise of snow.

– *the seasons*

We live by one
simple rule –
say it out loud
and it makes it true.

Living and dying
simultaneously;
my feet twist
and tangle
in the
blooming vines.

I spin
in the spotlight,
the white heat
beating down
the back
of my neck.

I twirl and leap
on the tips
of my toes,
trying to not teeter
on the edge,
in a tutu made
of diamond dust.

My toes bleed
beneath the silk,
the corset strains
my breathing;
but all at once
I feel your
fingertips
wrap tightly
around
my waist.

Suddenly
we're flying, and
I'm high in heaven,
for a moment,
till all at once
we sink back down
again –
you grab my hand
and drag me there.

I feel as if
I'm trapped
between,
not in limbo,
but some place else –
a place I've only
heard about,
but never truly seen.

– holy hell / en pointe

I can't rely on you
to feel anymore —
these streets don't speak
your name as clear.

What's gone is as distant
as the highways
we sped down so free;
what's closest is as warm
and safe as home.

The future smiles each day
as she greets me in the morning,
holding in her light
the promise of memories
worth writing about.

Open the window
to the backyard,
let the sunlight pour in,
let the lighter do its job;
drag the smoke into your lungs,
tell me every secret in your soul.

Order take-out,
close the door,
watch a movie
crisscross
on the floor;
hold me close,
tell me this is how
we'll always be.

Let the rain kiss the windows,
let your presence alone
lure me to sleep;
my little lullaby,
my warm beating heart,
promise here we'll always stay.

These four walls
hold our secrets,
your name etched under
the windowsill –
nothing here could ever change
and nothing ever will.

– *804*

There's a fine line
between art and life,
there's a fragile barrier
between dreams and reality.

The walls of the museum
hold something sacred and rare;
we disappear into its story,
its truth –
we blur the line
between what's real.

The breath of romance,
the way we fit together perfectly,
how we blend with the colors
to create something priceless
and pure –

we'll hold on forever
to this original masterpiece
we'll spend a lifetime creating
and eternity enjoying.

– *masterpiece*

Long mornings, drawn out days,
conversations filled with
the purest form of love.

Lazy afternoons,
stretching our bones,
the pathways and beds
we proudly call home.

To feel someone
so deep in your soul,
to want all of their time
wrapped in sunshine shadows
and rhymes.

To pour their coffee every morning
and maybe burn the toast
with sleepy eyes
and last night's ghost.

These days are ours to fill
with our lambent love,
to take our time unwinding
(our thoughts never strained),
to hold each other close
and never let go.

Someday
you'll open your window,
and savor the sun,
and finally realize
you were always the one.

– *one and only*

You were last seen
ripping out a page of my story,
sleeping under my sheets,
sleeping under the stars,
blowing in the breeze,
drifting in the dew,
forgetting my name,
and writing out something new,
smoking a cigarette behind a bar,
trespassing to take in some view,
dirt on your face,
mud on your shoes,
climbing a mountain,
scaling the sky,
sharing a smile,
and I don't know why.

– because I can't quite remember the last place I saw you

And in the end,
we were a train that stalled,
a momentum run out,
a book shut tight.

An impossible goodbye,
no place left
to run and hide;
my prayer unanswered,
the universe smiles
as it gently nudges me
towards the light.

Glimpses of the past
burn the backs of my eyes;
the warm tears
cleanse my soul.

Coming home to an empty place
(coming home) –
the future awaits.

A plane ticket unused,
broken, shattered plans;
cleaning the corners
and wiping away the dust –
the sun shines through the shutters:

I was so scared to lose you, but what I gained
will never compare.

Golden light
pours through the
open shutters,
the birds sing,
our lashes flutter.

The balmy breeze,
your warm legs on mine,
butterflies at the
windowsill –
there's nothing more divine.

Berry-stained fingertips,
your lips, my lips,
your lips –
sundresses for
undressing,
bumblebees, and
wind in the trees.

May we always know peace,
may our souls always grin,
may we never be afraid
to begin again.

– *summer skin*

I'm the gentle reminder,
the taste on your tongue,
the note that lingers
in every song sung.

I'm the tug on your shirt,
the sheet corner untucked,
the kind of thing
that tastes better after midnight.

I'm the flicker of a memory,
the first spring rain,
the skin and bones
of your fragile frame.

You're the wildflowers
beneath mountaintops,
I just want you to myself –
you and me
and no one else.

– *come find me*

I had a dream
you were the only one,
but awoke to find
myself alone.

My arms reached out,
my eyes wide open,
but nothing was there
as I was hoping.

And just when I thought
to return to my slumber,
I remembered exactly where
to find your number.

My heart flickered,
my mind recalled –
you're inside my chest,
you were there all along.

I remember when you loved me,
I remember when we danced the night away.
I remember drinks at midnight,
hungover all the next day.
You were younger, I was older,
we shared beds in every West Coast state;
sunshine dripping from your beach waves
and cherry lips from every snow cone taste.
I wish I knew then what I know now,
that some things are better left to time;
let them spark, and shine, and burn out
just for the thrill of the ride.
There's no use holding on to memories,
they'll fade just like the sun on the lake,
but I know I'll always remember
the summer you and I found too late.

I don't like goodbyes, so it was easier for me to pretend our silence was just an ellipsis instead.

How do you retrace
words unspoken
or rewrite the past?

Can you change the future
to rectify what's gone?

Will you store up the words
and keep them safe
to speak to me someday?

When fate crosses our paths,
in some distant dream,
I know, I know
we'll surely beam.

— words unspoken

The last full moon of the decade brought promise and hope;
the last full moon was a gentle reminder of a new day.
The soft, patient glow illuminated her silhouette and caught the strands of her hair.
The generous rain tumbled from the clouds, drop by drop, catching the leaves and the thunder in its path.
Bathed in moonlight, bathed in earnest, she knew quietly what the turn of the tide could bring.
So, she wrapped up her wishes, and her sunshine, and her soul, and she tied them together with a pretty pink bow to unravel and unveil when the world was ready.

– the last full moon of the decade

Masterpiece, work of art;
every feature, every curve
leaves me short of breath.

Turn me to stone,
carve out my flaws,
keep me in the light,
let the faces stare.

Trace your outline
with my thumb,
every touch
leaves me numb;

for when a pair
this sweet collides,
there's simply nothing
left to hide.

– masterpiece part ii

Skinny dip into my mind,
dive in head first;
hold your breath,
count to 10,
then follow the bubbles
to the surface.

Take a deep breath,
let the cool air
fill your lungs;
don't let the feeling leave
your lips
or your tongue.

Swim among the pools,
and scale the sudden
tidal waves;
learn to escape the riptides
unscarred and unscathed.

Navigate the waters
and learn how the tides
will turn;
float on your back to safety
and there you'll find me waiting.

Smoke curls
around
your lips,
the sunset catches
your breath
and the curve
of your neck.

The peachy hues
cling to your lashes
as the last of
the exhale
settles in
this empty room
and slowly
dissipates.

Like an old black
and white memory,
like the space
in this room,
will the love
we shared so
sweetly
vanish too?

Where the snow
meets the sea
is where you're sure
to find me.

Looking out into
the great beyond,
my secrets whispered
to the waves.

Tell me you won't
leave a trace,
no matter how brave
(you pretend to be).

Salt in the ocean,
salt in the street;
at the fine line of affection
is where we'll meet.

Nothing gained, nothing lost;
at least I'd like to think
it was happenstance
our paths crossed.

— *snow and the sea*

You've lived so many lives to have gotten you
here – your compass hasn't failed you yet,
and I don't think it ever will;
You found your way through the winding
country roads to your childhood home, so I
know you'll always find your way to me – the
path is worn and the flowers bloom big,
echoes and whispers that beckon you home.

– *backroads*

Cat on a windowsill,
peaches in a bucket;
open windows,
curtains billow,
the smell of dinner
drifts upstairs.

Freshly-picked flowers,
dirty dishes in the sink,
another bottle,
another sunset walk –
let the fireflies lead the way
(may these memories always stay).

Back porch swing,
crickets sweetly sing;
the soft promise
of a good night's sleep.

One more hit,
one more story;
it's us
who will cheat
the day.

Roses on gentle lips,
it's fate, it's timing,
it's your fingertips –

hold me close, and
keep me warm;
it's here that's where

we're safe from harm.

– *home*

Rest your head on my lap,
let it quiet and settle,
the day is nearly done,
let it set with the sun.

Work of art
with a ring of flowers
in your hair,
think only simple thoughts
like a slow dance
floats on air.

Let me gently pluck
the weeds and bugs
hidden just beneath
each calloused bud –

I'll leave nothing behind
but the sweet scent
of rose petals
and a place
for honey bees
to feel at ease.

– *slow dance*

You told me I was a light, that I was strong.
I told you I was lucky to have you,
that our souls fit together as one.
But now I'm just your ghost, or maybe
you're just mine,
because I still think back to you
time after time.

– the one that got away

Where are we?
Where did we run off to?

We were dancing in the wind,
speeding in a fast car
with our backs turned
towards the past.

How did we wash up
on the shores of a
nameless town
with the population
of the biggest city
in the smallest state?

How can we remember
tender nights on the highways
when we're sitting fireside
10,000 miles away?

I almost think
we've been here before,
but who's to say
when fragile memories
hit the floor each day?

– *the highway*

I store my suitcase on the shelf
to gently gather dust;
I softly wipe the stardust
out of my eyes
and gently tuck away
the memories
in a spot that is safe,
but hidden well.
Visions of mountains
and the smell of
sweet pines
lingers in my head;
I remember long days
and short nights
and sunsets from behind
the dirty dash.
I miss pit stops, and
pulling over,
and sweets
for the road.
Passing out in
parking lots
or a cheap room
for the night.
Views that shake you
to your core
and landscapes so lovely
it hurts.
I was a spirit
running wild
and free,
and in the middle of nowhere

I found myself.
I can simply remember
only a feeling now;
and in the middle of nowhere
I found what I was searching for.

– *the middle of nowhere*

You're one more kiss
before we part ways,
that look in your eyes
always makes me stay.

You're every backroad
that always leads me home;
back scratches before bed
wherever we roam.

You're the warmth of a fire
on a cold winter's night;
the sweetest soul,
love at first sight.

I'm your little spoon,
your starry sky,
the promise of summer,
and fireflies.

– I found you / come find me ii

He likes when my hair
smells like flowers
and it's not pulled back.

He likes when my bed
is messy, and we
wake up slow.

The stars share secrets
of how they string
the sky together,
and I can hear
your words
like dewdrops
in my ear.

Your lips taste
like honey,
and everything is fine;
the summer strawberries
are ripe and sweet
all along the vine.

– *bloom*

Sunday roast
and sweet tea –
you know everything
you mean to me.

Your hand on my thigh
speaks for itself;
we cruise into town
with the setting sun.

May our love never fade,
may we hold these memories close;
may we remember a time
when it was just us.

Broken sink tile,
broken hearts,
broken tears –
how did something,
once so fine
and rare,
end up
with cracks
in its design?

– dead flowers

The Ringmaster

It was a mundane day. It was the same routine I'd done for the past 100-plus days, over and over again. Hold this, hand this to you, point to the center of the main ring, present the main attraction, and clap and smile along with the applause of the crowd.

I finish the act, leave the tent, walk past the lions and the elephants, now in their cages, and waft away cigarette smoke from the ringmaster and the trapeze girls.

I make it to my tiny trailer, wipe off the silver glitter, and slowly pull off my fake eyelashes. I rub away what's left of my bright red lipstick and pull my hair back into a bun.

There's a knock on the door. It's the ringmaster. He opens the door a crack and tells me I did a good job today, just like he does every day after we finish the last show. He tips his tall, black top hat at me and closes the door.

I pick up my things and decide to take a trip into town for a bite to eat. On the way to the exit off the back lot, I decide to make a pit stop. I spot the ringmaster's trailer and walk up to the door to peer through the small window. I see he's not in. I slowly open the door and tiptoe inside.

I see it sitting in the corner on an overstuffed, plush chair. His black top hat sits tall and proud, but slightly worn around the edges, atop the seat cushion. I peer behind my shoulder to make sure no one is there and make a grab for it. I sneak out the door with the hat hidden behind my back and waltz into town, placing it proudly on my head when I'm out of sight from the trailers and the rest.

I make my way to a nearby diner and promptly order a cheeseburger, fries, onion rings, and a chocolate shake – a meal fit for a queen, the hat placed pompously on my head.

I take my time walking back, strolling through alleyways and backroads, walking tall and proud through the side streets. I'm the ringmaster now. I call the shots and run the show. I don't stand on the sidelines while someone else soaks up the spotlight and receives the applause.

They all look at me now. They come from their homes and pay their admission to see me and see what amazing feat I'll pull off next. No one overshadows me. I wear the top hat proudly and boldly.

I get back just before sunset and in time to place the hat back where it belongs without getting caught by anyone.

I quietly go back to my trailer and hang up my jacket on the hook next to the door. I make my way to lie down on the tiny twin bed and slowly drift to sleep, only to awake again and repeat the same day once more.

Wink

I threw my plans to the wayside
and rearranged my time.
I scooped up all the spontaneity
and finally made it mine.

I leapt and didn't look
and got behind the wheel,
left behind my restlessness,
all so I could feel.

Open roads, and soft
and gentle skies,
propellers standing tall,
swaying to the sighs.

4-3-2,
just for tonight;
sleeping next to you
was worth this plight.

7 AM,
east to west by dusk,
teetering on elation,
then no longer on the cusp.

Caught between a star
and a satellite,
silence I can bear,
promises delight.

Warm words
she'd bravely waited to hear;
traces of sweet pines
and melodies in her ear.

Catnaps
and chats;
three hours there,
three hours back.

Slowly snap to existence
and prolong confronting chores –
what's gone is mine,
and what's gone is yours.

I'm looking out into the garden
with a shyness in my eyes;
the evening glow comforts me,
the books pull me in.

You're standing just beyond the threshold
with bravery in your smile;
jasmine floats along the breeze,
fireflies linger at your hands.

To live or to die
would be the same in your arms;

to cross the threshold
or to embrace the warmth of home
would hold the same intimacy
as if we were one.

— one / the threshold

Spending summers in a nineteenth-century mansion, peeling paint on the walls, crickets chirping in the balmy breeze; twilight softly settles over the horizon and you take my hand up the creaking stairs. Homemade fun, homemade love – picnics in the parlor by the grand piano; the master bedroom our haven, the guest bedroom our reading room. Quiet nights spent drinking rose tea on the front porch, knowing the season will surely darken to the promise of changing leaves and barren trees. But all the while, clenching, holding on with everything we have to keep this slice of magic from breaking the illusion – but there's nothing we can do.

– *summer dreams*

The sunlight on my back
reminds me of you,
the silence in this room
reminds me we were true.

Caught between
the shadows and the light,
its distance changes
night to night.

The taste of your kiss
still lingers on my lips;
I miss your movements
and the rhythm of our hips.

So, scatter like sun rays,
and kiss the wildflowers on the way;
I wish with everything
you would just stay.

– stay / begging on my lips

These shy streets
hold more than
our memories;

as they settle down,
as the visitors move out,
fall quietly peeks its head in
and covers the buildings
with a golden glow.

The cool breeze blows
from the sea,
and I know these sleepy
streets are ours to keep.

Nothing has ever
felt sweeter
than the promise of autumn
and the elation,
the warmth
of two souls
dancing together
like the fireflies of fall,
never letting our feet
touch the ground.

You take me
by the hand,
we escape
the big band
and the glow
and sparkle
of the night;
my headband
is floppy,
the drinks
have us sloppy,
but we dance
till dawn
by the river.

You make fresh croissants,
my sweet tooth
is strong,
I smother them
in jam;
I watch you baking
each morning,
the rain's
always pouring;
we flirt
and we flicker,
we've never
been thicker,
but part ways
each evening
with a wink.

A psychedelic kiss,
spin the bottle,
and lover's bliss;
tie-dyed memories
and thick, humid nights,
lying naked in bed
by candlelit.

Our hearts
have traveled
through time,
through the universe
to get us here;
little steps
taken forward
till our time
finally came –
for true love,
for this love –
a love sweeter
than space.

– *time and the universe*

Even when the stars split and the waters cave, now that we're here, you'll always be with me.

Holding out to read
the very last page
of an already worn novel,
knowing I can never go back
to the dog-eared pages,
but knowing I'll never lay
the book to rest
on the highest shelf.

– *half-empty suitcase*

I once sat on the cool, white sand in the quiet of a small town with no one around for miles. I sat on the tall dunes with the sun setting before me and the moon rising behind me. The glow of the setting sun lit up the sky, the clouds ablaze and filled up with light. The orange-yellow glow reflected on my face and bathed the faraway ridges with its rays. The moon rose slowly behind me, proud, brilliant, and full. It lit up the darkness of the indigo sky over the distant mountains, its moonbeam radiance reflecting on the white sand, its light beams growing. I sat and wondered, to myself, in the silence, in the in-between, is this the part where the light from the sun will warm my skin and soothe my nerves as the world gently closes its eyes? Or has a planetarium of possibilities tumbled into the infinite and extraordinary abyss?

– the sun and the moon / afterlife

I followed the trail
of the red herring
deep
into
the woods
one night;

I followed
the pungent
smell
of the soft
earth.

A fool,
a hound
hungry in
the moonlight,
I searched
and sought,
but found
not a thing
to eat.

I try again,
night after night,
following the scent
down the rugged
path,
but
this time
I divert.

I catch
a faint
whiff
of something
more familiar,
something juicy,
something filling.

I struggle,
but I seek,
and I
patiently
follow
the trail

deep
into
the woods
one night.

I come upon
a shadow-filled
clearing,
and there
stands you
bathed in
the dreamiest
light
of the moon.

"What took you so long?"
you ask,

with a grin.

"You were hard to find,
and I got
distracted."

– *red herring*

We danced far away
from the symphony and the stage;
we held each other tight,
writing in our story another page.

We made up our own words
and savored every drop of rain;
we ran till our lungs couldn't take it,
but never felt the pain.

We dove into the deep end
and felt elation with every breath;
I swear I'll love you
and love you to death.

— *run*

Do you think the city smiled and waved as we drove away? With the sparkling lights in my rearview, do you think it winked and said, "I'll see you soon"? Do you think we could settle here and gently plant our roots, to one day blossom into something more lovely and fine? I think the city softly beckons and whispers our names, eagerly awaiting our return.

– the city

Love through the window
of a metro car in Paris,
passion blurs together
with the Eiffel Tower's reflection –

so sacred
and lonely, but
everlasting
nonetheless;
its afterglow
stirs us
in this brilliant mess.

Twist your bones
to fit my frame,
muddy the line
between what's real
and what plays tricks
on our minds.

Did we speed past
our most precious moments
and forget to write them down?
Or were they never
really beautiful
and just riding the metro
alone instead?

– *metro car in Paris*

Let's set sail,
and let the wind
guide us home.

Let's hold our gazes steady
as the waves rock us
to and from.

Nothing so merciless
and nothing so vast
could ever be enough
to shake the anchor
or re-write the past.

— *dream boat*

We got off the
train together,
never left the
side of the other.

We roamed the city,
talked non-stop,
and shared two cups
of coffee.

We spilled our secrets,
talked of simple things,
laughed too hard,
and slept too soundly.

We knew what we had
was full of whimsy,
full of magic,
and authenticity –

something that can't
be replicated,
not even
for a
second.

– *rare*

Kiss me on the street corner
when your arms are full of bread;
let's wander into a café
and slyly steal a taste.

Toss some coins
to a mandolin player
playing on the avenue,
drift home in the winter sun
with nothing but cares
to leave behind.

This classic love,
your vintage bomber –
this black and white adoration
was made to last a lifetime.

– the Parisian apartment

Balancing on the cusp
of dusk and dawn,
the moonlight
languorously pours
through the shutters;
I can only make out
the contour of your body,
the curve of your hips.

Kisses like honeysuckles
blooming in spring,
holding our breaths,
anxiously waiting for rain.

Silhouette daydream,
carry us away on the breeze;
chlorine lingers in your hair,
tangerine on your fingertips.

Promise we'll never break the spell,
promise the sun will never rise;
just hold me in your
warm, forbearing arms
until time has run out
and our memories fade.

– *fool's paradise*

You don't have to imagine a world without me in it – it's you and me against it.

– don't know what I'd do without you

Do I swim into the ocean
without the stars to guide me?
Do I wade the waters
unknowingly
and hold my breath
as its waters crash?

The echo of a song
from a shell,
the salt and the sea,
its pungent smell;

Learning how to become one
with the vast, hungry tides,
floating and flailing
until the waves subside.

The sirens may sing
and the sailors may listen,
but fancy fallacies
often glisten.

– *the siren*

Sew your name
into the hem of
our love;
stitch it safely
and thread it
with care –

what's written
on our souls
is, at times,
much to bear.

Trace the letters
with ease;
if you want to
come in to
my heart,
I'll hand you
the keys.

No need for knocking,
no need to make noise,
sitting in silence with
you is a simple joy.

– simple joys

Fresh fruit from the market sits proudly in a porcelain bowl on the kitchen table.
The magpies sing outside the bathroom window as daylight fills the sky.
Our sun-soaked living room scatters dust between the light.
The books sit idle on the shelf, waiting to be cracked open for an afternoon delight.
Two pairs of blue eyes gently open to welcome the day;
long eyelashes flutter and fall as sleepy limbs wrap around one another.
One gentle kiss and one stolen glance is our secret promise to stay in bed just a little longer.

– scenes from Sunday mornings

Hold me again
with only your gaze,
tell me not to go
when I'm halfway
down the hall.

Save the supermarket
flowers –
all I need
is your touch;
cradle your face,
hold on to our fate –
we're on our way now.

We'll sail to
the moon
in a sea full
of stars,
we'll conquer
the waves and
the mountaintops.

If this little apartment
is all we have,
may it keep
our love safe,
may we always
know warmth.

I can almost hear you call,
I can almost hear you scream,
I can almost hear you tiptoe
back to my door.

My bedsheets stay messy,
the shutters swung open;
I remember the day you left,
your car disappearing down the drive.

I miss the smell of coffee
floating up the stairs,
I miss your blue eyes
and adoring stare.

All that's left
is me
and the singing trees;
how could something
so beautiful,
so free,
slip from my hands so easily?

– *the window*

We'd shine as brightly as the streetcars
crossing the Champs-Élysés.
We'd twirl under streetlamps in winter coats
with stars sewn in the hem.
We'd wander aimlessly up and down the
tree-lined avenues until our heads are
spinning from the madness and the magic.
As darkness rests its sleepy head on the
sparkling city, we'd wander into a café for
after-dinner coffee and croissants.
The city would sing our love song back to us
as we stumble in its stupor, our wide-eyed
gazes never leaving the other.

– we'll always have Paris

Pick up the phone
in our corner of the world,
let me hear your voice
and picture your face
next to mine.

Hold me with your strong arms
and whisper honey in my ears;
let the rose petals fall,
let there be no more tears.

Paint our story
with colors that remind us
of the sun,
sketch every detail,
don't let the
watercolors run.

Being with you
could never be more tender,
but long nights on the phone
has its splendor.

– *ring*

You left me in a bar
where third meets St. Marks
with lipstick on my glass
and a barely lit spark.

The sting in my throat
wasn't enough
to wash out the taste
of your kiss;

the thousands of
good-looking men
offering me a light
weren't enough
to keep me warm at night.

Say what you will
and do what you must –
this city was never
huge enough
for two hearts like us.

– *speak easy*

I owe my debts to the canyon
and my time to the sea;
the redwoods whisper your name
with every branch of their tree.

The mountains in their splendor
beam with wildflowers and snow;
I'll always remember
the words that they spoke.

The deserts kiss the sun,
and the crags strike the sky;
on each sunset and silence
I could always rely.

But nothing is as simple
and nothing is more free
as when you turn around
and whisper, "Come with me."

— *the landscape / the adventure*

Sunset lullaby;
roads with no names –
highway drifters,
states with different times.
Slowly drifting
into the night
unsure of where
the sun meets the sky.
Bones that ache,
hearts that shake –
heavy lids
and half-full stomachs.
A smile with a stranger,
never exchanging names;
the sweet impact
of a simple life.
Wide open sky –
two hearts on the run
aching to grasp
what was always meant as theirs.

Black and white
summer classics
at the theatre
downtown –
the marquee lights
placing soft,
glowing halos
above our heads.

Fireworks out west
gently popping
over the hills,
the summer breeze
softly carrying
our hair
with it
as we cling
to each other
in the balm
of the night.

Packing boxes,
slowly unpacking boxes
as a new space
takes shape;
the crickets hum
in the gloom,
the massive stars
outshine the moon,
our lips collide –
never too soon.

Smooth rides
into town
with the windows
rolled low;
ice cream cones
and sticky fingers –
I'll never forget
this moment.

– how summer passed part ii

I saw you here once. Twice, maybe.
Sipping a cocktail with a friend,
ordering another at the bar, smoking a
cigarette out back just before calling it
a night.

Plush pink chairs, the golden, peachy-
sunset radiance behind the counter –
just one glance at the other was
enough to make the room disappear.
Your rosy cheeks called my hopeful
eyes to the other side of the room and
so began a night that shimmered and
glowed.

A bit of stardust on both of our lips, we
shared a drink, we made a toast. You
took my hand in yours, we danced and
twirled until the room was blurry, and
we needed another martini to calm us
down. We spoke in confidence of
mystery, lust, and illusions, your
emerald greens never leaving mine.
With a gleam in your smile and a glint
in your story, you tore out a page just
for me. You left your name on a bit of
crumpled napkin with whiskey on
your breath and my lipstick stain on
the corner – you told me to look you
up. You slid out the back door just as
soon as you'd come, leaving nothing

behind but the distant echo of departure.

The whispers say you left town, they say
we'll never know where you ran off to or
where your ghost goes, but I know it's inside
these baby pink walls where madness stirs
and clever comebacks flourish. Where you
left your mark and lost your mind, if only for
a night.

I feel your presence in every sip of my
cosmopolitan, I see your face on every well-
dressed stranger. I sit in our corner booth,
almost nightly they say, waiting for you to
show your beaming face, my sorrow hidden
behind the notes of a Sinatra tune. But
delusions and fantasies only float so far until
they disappear to wherever you are.

– the man

Pretty as a painting,
we're sleepwalking
in the rain,
the end of the sunset
on the tip of your cigarette.

We're dreaming together,
the neon glow
of the humming city –
the entrance to it all.

Its bluish-light splendor
could cradle me to sleep,
but the dreamy brilliance
of the sidewalks and streets
endlessly stirs my thoughts.

Let's succumb to its spell,
may we stop and always stare,
the opulence of the night
luring us from our slumber.

Even when we can't sleep,
may we still have the chance to dream.

– *Tokyo*

Someday when our record collections
combine,
when what's mine is yours and yours is
mine,
when the sunlight pours through the
windows on the hardwood floors,
we'll hold each other close as the vinyl spins
and flowers blossom in the sun of spring,
butterflies fluttering,
carrying with them
unadulterated peace.

– *butterflies*

Another night out,
another subway ride,
another last call,
another, "I just might."

Stairway to heaven,
kiss me with roses on
your breath;
time holds for applause
as we slowly near
our fate.

Another messy bed,
another messy head,
another sweet slumber,
another can't-lose-your-number.

The record spins without sound,
the rain slowly tumbles down;
when it gets this good,
you're bound to lose your mind.

– *tunnel vision*

Mayhem and magic,
mischief and shadows –
these snow-covered streets,
this streetlamp glow
leads us down
roads unknown.

The soft patter
of freezing rain
lingers deep
into the woods.

Fresh tracks,
midnight radiance,
the moon
and the wolves
could never
find us here.

Wrap me in
your capable arms,
and kiss
my frostbit lips;

reality melts
like the snow
with my skin beneath
your fingertips.

– *snow*

It's 2 AM in this shoddy diner, and the sleep
is starting to show in your eyes. You haven't
even touched your slice of apple pie, but all I
can think about is how the color of the coffee
matches the brown in your eyes, how the soft
neon glow of the "open" sign is softly
reflecting in your tousled golden locks.
I hold my head like it's midnight instead
(like it makes any difference), but you insist
on resting yours in the palm of your hand.
The look on your face says, "Let's get out of
here and find a real party to enjoy," but the
cigarette on your breath says, "Maybe we can
stay, just a little bit longer."

– *James Dean*

Drunk
and dizzy
off glistening
city lights

perched
and peppered
in the
cobalt night sky.

The honey
and heavy
gravity
of longings.

Sweet salutations
of crickets
in the warm
and balmy breeze.

— *Sunday joyride*

Cotton candy skies;
the glow of his smile
plays tricks on my mind
as it catches the sunset.

Salty air, sticky fingers,
little lies, and little sins.
Our hands fit like poetry,
and our lips lock
like a key in a hole.

Hazy air, hazel eyes;
deep pools of wonder,
yet full of lies.

Two ships
no better off apart;
two sailors
without a lighthouse
to guide them home.

Rocky waves, silent prayers;
the folded-up pictures
from the day we met
will carry us through
to our final days afloat.

— *pink dreams*

The child in me
is running in a field
with all her cares behind her.

She can't see beyond the horizon,
but she doesn't need to
to know that everything
will be ok.

She is patient,
and forgiving,
and tries her best
to chase after the sun
and fill the spaces in her soul.

She's proud of the flowers
growing around her
and tends to the bugs and the weeds.

She'll make light of
the ephemeral storms
and greet each rainbow with hope.

She may sometimes need
a hand to hold
or a shoulder to cry on,
but her vigor and courage
can clear any sky.

– *clear skies*

Crisscross in your oversized,
hand-me-down flannel,
soft rain and a cool breeze
outside the window panels.

Quiet mornings,
homemade breakfast,
orange juice, and coffee;
perfect peace at last.

Sunday cartoons,
stay in bed for hours,
a sanctuary, an island
faraway from showers.

Mornings with you,
lambent light from the sunrise;
a letter opened at the creases
for only our eyes.

– *mornings with you*

Like a love song sung in unison,
our sweet, saccharine voices
carry down slick city streets.

Ambling over bridges
soaked in city lights,
the historic buildings
smile down on us,
the starry night
holds its reign.

The poetry around every corner
overwhelms your senses,
the romance of it all
follows closely behind.

To see the whole universe
reflected in your eyes
a thousand miles from home,
to hold our gazes steady
wherever we'll roam.

– *love song*

You broke my heart
in a million ways,
but I broke it too
by simply loving you.

We rode the train,
I didn't look back,
we talked outside the party,
we shared our stories.

I wanted you to call
with no hesitation,
I wanted to answer
and spill our souls.

I never meant
for it to end this way,
but my calloused,
tired heart couldn't
get past its pride.

I wanted
to hear your words,
but I couldn't
practice compassion.

You're not a bother,
and I love that you try –
I should've listened
before the whole well
ran dry.

To be with you in love,
to heed its sweet sigh,
to fall into its dreamlike state
and never wonder why.

To know that we are infinite,
that nothing could sever our ties,
connections and reflections
in the skies of your eyes.

Send my senses reeling
at the hill atop the city;
fill my lungs with wildflowers
and something strangely pretty.

Falling could never be more effortless
with you to keep me safe;
our language of love always yields
to something stronger than faith.

We wore out the words "I love you" like the spine of an old book, our story read over and over again.

Table of Contents

Intro   page 4
Two wildflowers   page 7
The garden   page 9
To carry   page 11
Mess   page 13
The big top   page 15
Your song   page 17
Fall magic   page 19
Petrichor   page 21
Matching birthmarks   page 23
Summer house   page 25
Snow up to my knees   page 27
Teacups   page 29
Sin city   page 31
Single   page 33
Young love   page 35
Morning rain   page 37
Center St. at sunset   page 39
Just a feeling   page 41
Cigarette   page 43
Scissors   page 45
The kiss   page 46
Museum   page 49
Brand new   page 51
Fall   page 53
Coffee shop ghosts   page 55
Float   page 57
Forever   page 59
Breakfast on the front porch   page 61
Baby cut his own hair   page 63

Fleeting moments page 65
Smeared ink page 67
Midnight rider page 69
English sky page 71
Lost summer page 73
Salad days page 75
Forever ii page 77
Indian summer page 78
Dusk page 80
I whisper your name page 83
To my younger self page 85
The seasons page 87
The rule page 89
Holy hell page 90
I can't rely on you page 93
804 page 95
Masterpiece page 97
Long mornings page 99
One and only page 101
Last seen page 103
In the end page 105
Summer skin page 107
Come find me page 109
I had a dream page 111
I remember page 113
Silence page 115
Words unspoken page 117
The last full moon page 119
Masterpiece part ii page 121
Skinny dip page 123
Smoke curls page 125
Snow and the sea page 127

Backroads   page 129
Home   page 130
Slow dance   page 133
The one that got away   page 135
The highway   page 137
The middle of nowhere   page 138
I found you/come find me   page 141
Bloom   page 143
Sunday roast   page 145
Dead flowers   page 147
The Ringmaster   page 148
Wink   page 152
One/the threshold   page 155
Summer dreams   page 157
Stay/begging on my lips   page 159
These shy streets   page 161
Time and the universe   page 162
Even when   page 165
Half-empty suitcase   page 167
The sun and the moon   page 169
Red herring   page 170
Run   page 175
The city   page 177
Metro car in Paris   page 179
Dream boat   page 181
Rare   page 183
The Parisian apartment   page 185
Fool's paradise   page 187
Our world   page 189
The siren   page 191
Simple joys   page 193
Scenes from Sunday   page 195

Hold me again   page 197
The window   page 199
We'll always have Paris   page 201
Ring   page 203
Speak easy   page 205
The landscape/the adventure page 207
Sunset lullaby   page 209
How summer passed part ii   page 210
The man   page 212
Tokyo   page 215
Butterflies   page 217
Tunnel vision   page 219
Snow   page 221
James Dean   page 223
Sunday joyride   page 225
Pink dreams   page 227
Clear skies   page 229
Mornings with you   page 231
Love song   page 233
Dry   page 235
To be with you in love   page 237
143   page 239

Acknowledgments

Thank you to everyone who has encouraged and inspired me to keep writing and to write a second collection of poems.

Thank you to my parents and my sister for keeping me on my toes and being excited about my work. To my mom for your eye for detail and creative spirit, my dad for your passion and support, and my sister for always pushing me to be my best.

To my lovely boyfriend, the best poems are always for you, one way or another. You're always with me, and you're ever-present in the pages of this book. Thanks for making each chapter of my life even brighter.

To my readers, thank you for your support. It means everything, and I hope you were able to connect in some way to my pieces. Stay tuned for more.

About Me

Noelle is a graduate of the University of Texas where she studied Journalism.
She's loved creating and telling stories from a very young age and currently resides in Austin, where she grew up. She enjoys reading, writing, and traveling the world in her free time.
This is Noelle's second collection of poetry. Check out her first collection, "Night Swimming," for more beautiful words.

Contact:

noelledarilek@gmail.com

Instagram:

@noellewritespoetry

Printed in Great Britain
by Amazon